PowerPoint
2000

QUICK FIX

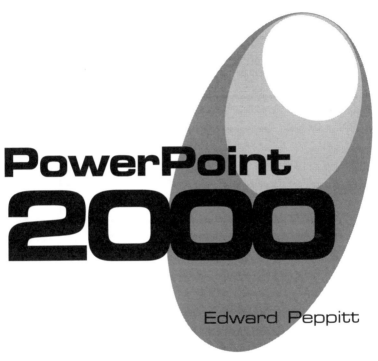

PowerPoint
2000

Edward Peppitt

QUICK FIX

TEACH YOURSELF BOOKS

For UK orders: please contact Bookpoint Ltd, 130 Milton Park, Abingdon, Oxon OX14 4SB. Telephone: (44) 01235 400414, Fax: (44) 01235 400454. Lines are open 9.00 - 6.00, Monday to Saturday, with a 24-hour message answering service. E-mail: orders@bookpoint.co.uk

British Library Cataloguing in Publication Data
A catalogue record for this title is available from the British Library.

First published 2001 by Hodder Headline Plc, 338 Euston Road, London, NW1 3BH.

Typeset by Butford Technical Publishing, Birlingham, Worcs.
Printed in Great Britain for Hodder & Stoughton Educational, a division of Hodder Headline Plc, 338 Euston Road, London NW1 3BH by Cox & Wyman, Reading, Berkshire.

Impression number   10 9 8 7 6 5 4 3 2 1
Year 2006 2005   2004   2003   2002   2001

Contents

CONTENTS

VIII

CONTENTS

Getting Started

Start PowerPoint 2000

1 Click **Start**.

2 Point to **Programs**.

3 Select **Microsoft PowerPoint**.

OR

Double-click Microsoft PowerPoint on your desktop.

Close PowerPoint 2000

1 Click on **✕** in top right-hand corner of screen.

   OR

   In the **File** menu, select **Exit**.

2 Save your document(s) if you are prompted to do so.

Create a new blank presentation

1 Start PowerPoint.

2 Select **Blank presentation** if prompted to do so.

3 Click **OK**.

OR

1 Click 🏁 **Start**.

2 Select **New Office Document**.

3 Select **Blank presentation**.

4 Click **OK**.

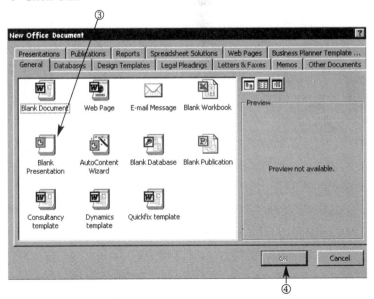

Create a new presentation using a template

1 Start PowerPoint.

2 In the **File** menu, select **New**.

④   ③

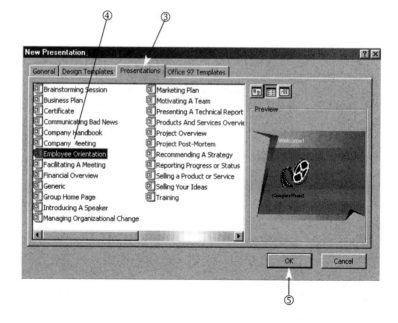

⑤

3 Click on the tab for the type of presentation that you want to create.

4 Select a template.

5 Click **OK**.

tip

PowerPoint comes with a range of common templates preloaded. To create your own templates, or amend existing ones, see the section on Templates.

Create a new presentation using AutoContent Wizard

1 Start PowerPoint.

2 Select **AutoContent Wizard** if prompted to do so.

OR

1 In the **File** menu, select **New**.

2 Select **AutoContent Wizard** and click **OK**.

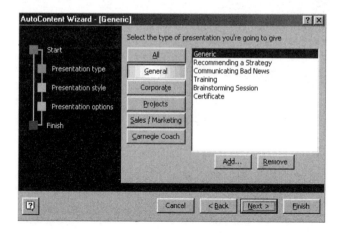

3 Follow the Wizard's step-by-step instructions to create your presentation.

4 Click **Finish** when you have completed the last instruction.

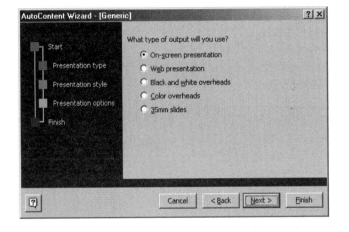

Open an existing presentation

GETTING STARTED

1 Click .

   OR

   In the **File** menu, select **Open**.

2 Navigate to the folder containing the presentation you want to open.

3 Double-click on the presentation.

   OR

   Click once on the presentation and then click 📂 Open .

> **tip**
>
> If you want to open a document that you have worked on recently, you may see it listed at the foot of the File menu. If so, just click on it to select it.

Close a presentation

Click on the lower close button in the top-right hand corner of the PowerPoint screen.

OR

In the **File** menu, select **Close**.

You may wish to save your work if you are prompted to do so.

Click to
close

Find a presentation

It is very easy to forget where on your hard disk you have saved a presentation. If this happens to you:

1 Click **Start** and select **Find**, then **Files** or **Folders**.

2 Enter the name of the presentation, or a part of it.

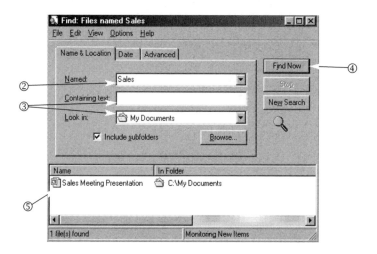

3 Add any other data that might assist the search process into the appropriate fields (e.g. a date range or some keywords contained in the text).

4 Click **Find Now**.

5 Files matching the search criteria will be listed.

6 Double-click on the file name to open it.

Screen Display

Change the way a document is displayed

PowerPoint provides five different ways of viewing your work. To switch between views, click on one of the view buttons in the bottom left-hand corner of your screen.

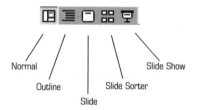

Normal

Outline

Slide

Slide Sorter

Slide Show

Normal View

The Normal View divides the screen into the slide, notes and slide outline panes. This view allows you to work on all the common parts of a presentation within one screen.

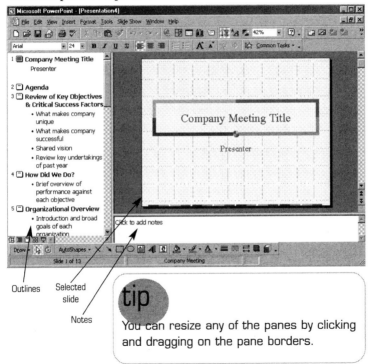

Outlines

Selected slide

Notes

tip

You can resize any of the panes by clicking and dragging on the pane borders.

Outline View

The Outline View is ideal when you are working on the text content of the slides in your presentation. A thumbnail of the slide is displayed, but most of the display is devoted to the text contained within each slide. There is also a smaller pane to add notes.

Slide thumbnail

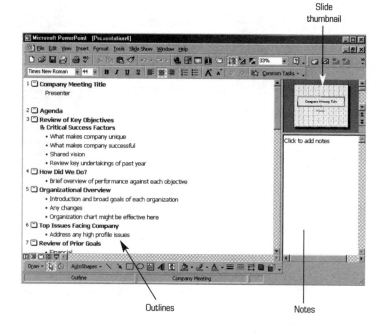

Outlines

Notes

Slide View

Use the Slide View to preview how each slide looks. Click on a slide number in the left-hand panel to go straight to that slide. You can also rearrange slides in this view, by clicking and dragging a slide number in the left-hand panel to a new position.

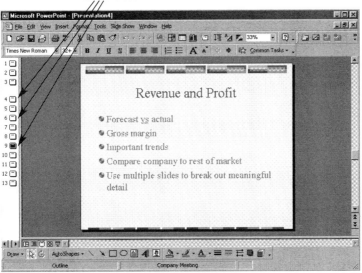

Click to go straight to these slides

Slide Sorter View

Use the Slide Sorter View when you want to add transitions,
animations or other effects to your slides. You can also rearrange
slides quickly and easily in Slide Sorter View.

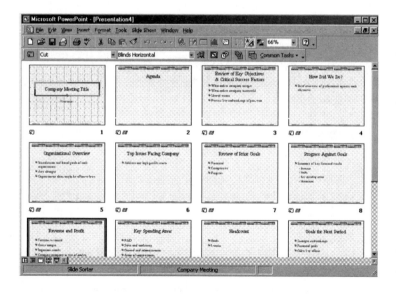

Slide Show View

The Slide Show View displays each slide in turn, exactly the way it will appear in the finished presentation. Use this view to run through your presentation, rehearse timings and check your presentation.

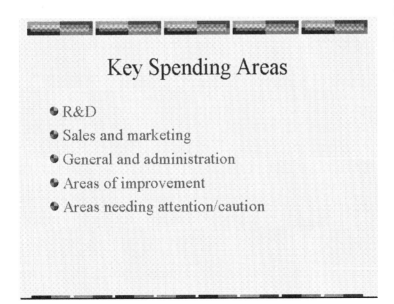

Display/hide a toolbar

1 In the **View** menu, point to **Toolbars**.

2 Click to select the toolbar that you want to display/hide.

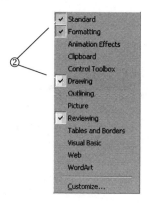

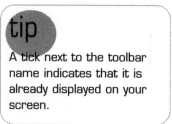

tip

A tick next to the toolbar name indicates that it is already displayed on your screen.

Display the ruler

1 Make sure that you are in either Normal or Slide View.

Normal View

2 In the **View** menu, select **Ruler**.

tip

To hide the ruler, repeat steps 1 and 2 above.

Switch between open presentations

If you have two or more presentations open at the same time, you can switch quickly and easily between them.

In the **Window** menu, select the file name for the presentation that you want to switch to.

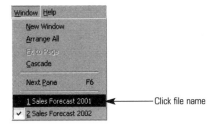

Click file name

OR

Click on the appropriate file name in the Windows taskbar.

Click file name

Show the Office Assistant

The Office Assistant is an animated character that sits on your desktop. If the Office Assistant is running, help is available via the character's speech bubble. The Office Assistant will also offer tips and advice based on what you are doing in PowerPoint.

You can specify the way in which the Office Assistant provides help.

1 In the **Help** menu, select **Show the Office Assistant**.

2 Click on the Office Assistant.

3 Click **Options**.

4 Click on the **Options** tab.

5 Click to select the options you require.

6 Click **OK**.

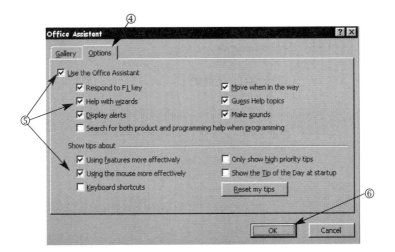

Use the Office Assistant

1 Click on the Office Assistant.

2 Type a question and click **Search**.

3 Select from the range of answers provided.

4 You will now be taken to specific help.

Turn off the Office Assistant

Many users find the Office Assistant irritating, and you may wish to turn this feature off.

1 Click on the Office Assistant.

2 Click **Options**.

3 Click on the **Options** tab.

4 Click once to remove the tick in **Use the Office Assistant**.

tip

You can also turn off the Office Assistant by right-clicking on the Office Assistant, and selecting Hide. But if you do this, the Office Assistant will return next time you open any Microsoft Office program!

Use the Help command

The Help command is more useful if the Office Assistant is turned off.

1 In the **Help** menu, select **Microsoft PowerPoint Help**.

   OR

   Press **[F1]**.

2 Click on the **Contents** tab to see the range of help topics available. Double-click on a topic, select an individual query, and the help will appear in the preview screen on the right of the Help dialog box.

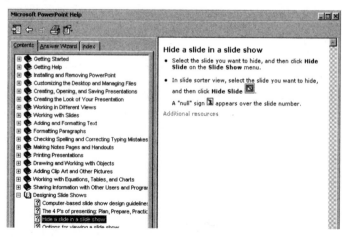

3 Click on the **Answer Wizard** tab if you have a specific question. Type in the question, then select a topic to display.

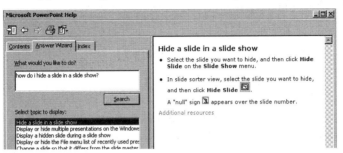

4 Click on the **Index** tab to enter a keyword of your own, or to select a keyword from the alphabetical list. Help relating to the keyword will then be displayed.

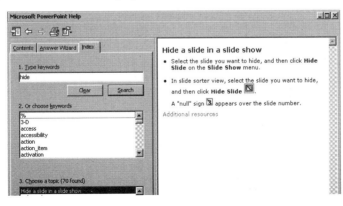

Use the What's This? command

HELP

1 In the **Help** menu, select **What's This?**

   OR

   Hold down **[Shift]** and press **[F1]**.

2 The mouse pointer will turn into a question mark.

3 Click on a feature within PowerPoint for a quick help summary.

For example, if you click on a toolbar command, a caption summarizes the command's functionality.

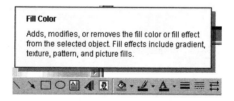

Detect and repair problems

If you suspect that PowerPoint is not running as it should, you will often find that the **Detect and Repair** function will sort the problem out.

1 In the **Help** menu, select **Detect and Repair**.

2 Click **Start**.

3 Insert the CD with PowerPoint 2000 on it when prompted to do so.

4 If a fault is found, select **Repair Office**.

5 Choose either to **Reinstall Office** or **Repair Errors in Your Office Installation**.

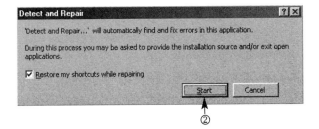

Save

Save a presentation for the first time

1 Click 🖫 on the standard toolbar.

2 Navigate to the folder where you wish to store the presentation.

3 Give the presentation a meaningful name.

4 Click **Save**.

Save a presentation

You should remember to save your document at regular intervals in one of the following ways:

- Click 🖫 at any time.

- In the **File** menu, select **Save**.

- Hold down **[Ctrl]** and press **[S]**.

Save a presentation as a different file type

1 In the **File** menu, select **Save As**.

2 Click on the down arrow next to **Save as type**.

3 Select an appropriate file type.

4 Click **Save**.

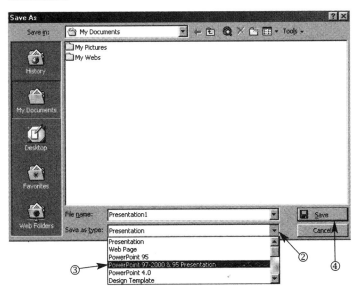

Save a copy of a presentation

1 Open the presentation that you want to copy.

2 In the **File** menu, select **Save As**.

3 Navigate to the directory where you want to store the copy.

4 Rename the document.

5 Click **Save**.

Save a slide as a graphic image

1 In the **File** menu, select **Save As**.

2 Click to select the **Save as type** drop-down menu.

3 Select a suitable graphics format (e.g. JPEG or GIF).

4 Enter an appropriate file name.

5 Click **Save**.

6 Click **Yes** to save all slides in the presentation, or **No** to save only the current slide.

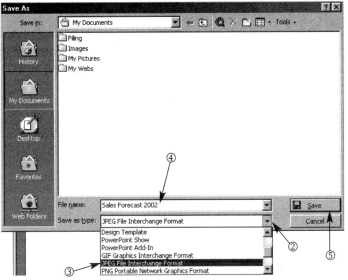

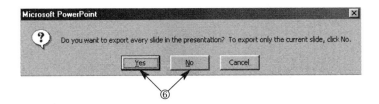

Fundamentals

Insert a new slide

1 Click on 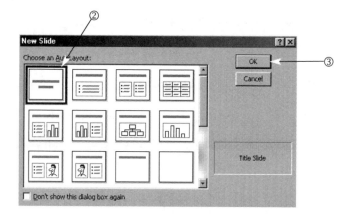.

2 Select a suitable AutoLayout.

3 Click **OK**.

OR

1 In the **Insert** menu, select **New Slide**.

2 Select a suitable AutoLayout.

3 Click **OK**.

Duplicate a slide

1 Make sure you are in Outline View.

2 Click on the slide that you wish to duplicate.

3 In the **Edit** menu, select **Duplicate**.

The new slide appears straight after the slide duplicated.

Apply an AutoLayout to an existing slide

1 Display the slide whose layout you wish to format.

2 Make sure you are in Normal or Slide View.

3 Click on Common Tasks ▾.

4 Select **Slide Layout**.

5 Select a suitable AutoLayout.

6 Click **Apply**.

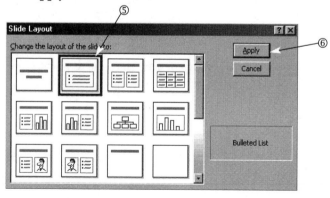

Select an object

1 Move the mouse pointer over the object, until the pointer changes to an arrow with four heads.

2 Click once.

A frame appears around the object to indicate that it is selected.

tip

To select several objects at the same time, hold down **[Shift]** whilst clicking on each object in turn.

Deselect an object

Click outside the border of the selected object.

Border of
selected object

Move an object

1 Move the mouse pointer over the object, until the pointer changes to an arrow with four heads.

2 Click once to select it.

3 Hold down the mouse and drag the object to the new location.

OR

1 Move the mouse pointer over the object, until the pointer changes to an arrow with four heads.

2 Click once to select it.

3 Use the arrow keys to move the object to the new location.

Delete an object

1 Move the mouse pointer over the object, until the pointer changes to an arrow with four heads.

2 Click once to select the object.

3 Press **[Delete]**.

Text

Enter text on the slide

Each PowerPoint slide contains text placeholders ready for your use.

1 Click inside the text placeholder.

2 Type in text as required.

3 Click outside the text placeholder to deselect it.

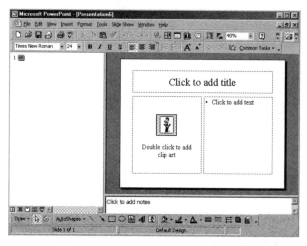

Enter text in an outline

You can develop the text content of your presentation by switching to Outline View.

1 Switch to Outline View.

2 Click where you want the text to appear.

3 Enter text as required.

4 Press **[Enter]** at the end of each line.

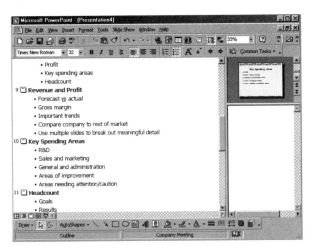

Create a text box

1 In the **View** menu, point to **Toolbars** and select **Drawing**.

2 Click on .

3 Click and drag mouse to draw a text box.

4 Release the mouse.

5 Click inside the text box and start typing.

Format a text box

1 Click on the text box frame to select it.

2 Right-click and select **Format Text Box**.

tip

You can also resize the text box by clicking and dragging the sizing handles around the frame.

3 You can format the size, colour and position of the text box.

4 Click **OK**.

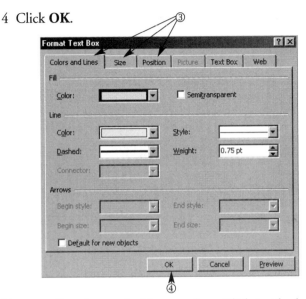

You can align the text inside a text box. Click inside the text box, and select one of the text alignment icons.

Left   Centre   Right
align   align

Cut text

1 Highlight the text to be cut.

2 Click ✂.

Copy text

1 Highlight the text to be copied.

2 Click 📋.

Paste text

1 Move the cursor to where the text will be inserted.

2 Click 📋.

tip

There are keyboard shortcuts to make cut, copy and paste even quicker:

[Ctrl] and [X] = cut

[Ctrl] and [C] = copy

[Ctrl] and [V] = paste

Make two or more copy selections

1 In the **View** menu, select **Toolbars**, then **Clipboard**.

2 Highlight first copy selection, then click in the Clipboard toolbar.

3 Highlight next copy selection, then click 📋 in the Clipboard toolbar.

4 You can make up to twelve copy selections in this way.

5 Click 📋 Paste All to paste all copy selections in the same place.

   OR

Click on the appropriate icon to paste an individual copy selection.

tip

You can use the Office Clipboard in this way to copy content between Microsoft Office software applications.

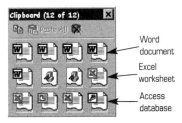

Word document

Excel worksheet

Access database

Set tabs

1 In the **View** menu, point to **Toolbars** and select **Ruler**.

2 Click inside the paragraph whose tabs you wish to set.

3 Click the tab button to set the type of tab that you want to set.

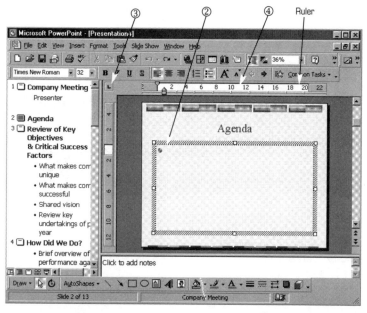

4 Click on the ruler at the point where you want the tab to
appear.

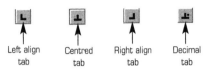

| Left align tab | Centred tab | Right align tab | Decimal tab |

Clear tabs

Click and drag the tab away from the ruler.

Indent text

1 Switch to Outline View.

2 Click to select the text that you want to indent.

3 Click where indicated to increase or decrease the indent level.

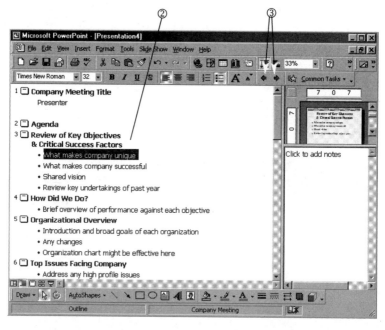

Add a shadow to text

1 Click to select the text that you want to shadow.

2 Click 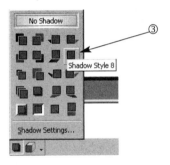 on the Drawing toolbar.

3 Click to select a suitable shadow style.

Text with shadow

Progress Against Goals

Formatting

Create a bulleted or numbered list

1 Highlight the text that you want to be bulleted or numbered.

2 Click on the appropriate icon in the formatting toolbar.

Numbers   Bullets

Create a bulleted or numbered list as you type

1 Move the cursor to the point where you want a bulleted or numbered list.

2 Click on the appropriate icon in the formatting toolbar (see opposite).

3 Begin typing.

4 Create a new bulleted or numbered point by pressing **[Enter]**.

tip

Click on the bullet or number icon for a second time to deselect when you have finished your list.

Customize bullets and numbers

1 Highlight the numbered or bulleted list.

2 In the **Format** menu, select **Bullets and Numbering**.

3 Select an appropriate number or bullet style.

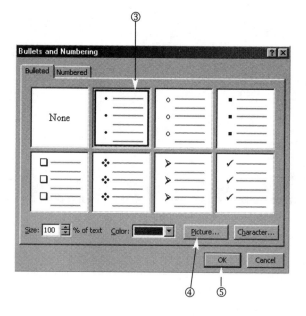

4 Click 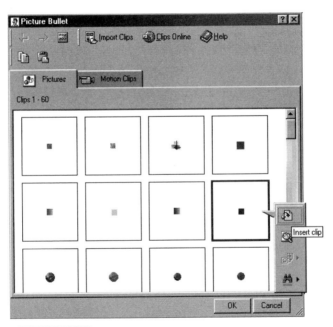 Picture... for other bullet options.

5 Click **OK**.

PICTURE BULLET STYLES

Undo a bulleted or numbered list

1 Highlight the bulleted or numbered list.

2 Click on the appropriate icon in the formatting toolbar.

Numbers   Bullets

OR

1 Highlight the bulleted or numbered list.

2 In the **Format** menu, select **Bullets and Numbering**.

3 Select **None**.

Alter paragraph line spacing

1 Click inside the paragraph whose line spacing you want to alter.

2 In the **Format** menu, select **Line Spacing**.

3 Set the required spacing.

4 Click **OK**.

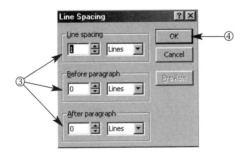

Select text using the mouse

To select a word:

- Double-click the word.

To select a range of text:

- Click and hold while dragging the mouse over the text.

Drag and drop text (move)

You can move text around a document using the drag and drop feature.

1 Highlight the text to be moved.

2 Click on the highlighted text and move to desired position.

3 Release the mouse.

Drag and drop text (copy)

1 Highlight the text to be copied.

2 Hold down **[Ctrl]** key, click on highlighted text and move to desired position.

3 Release the mouse.

Format text

1 Highlight the text that you want to format.

2 Use the tools on the Formatting toolbar as required.

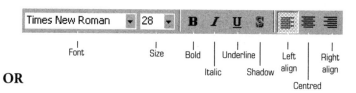

Font	Size	Bold	Underline	Left	Right
			align|align
	Italic	Shadow	
		Centred

OR

1 In the **Format** menu, select **Font**.

2 Make other changes as required.

3 Click **OK**.

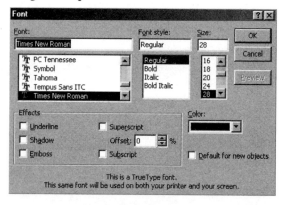

Align text

1 Highlight the text that you want to align.

2 Click on the appropriate icon in the Formatting toolbar.

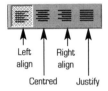

Left
align

Right
align

Centred   Justify

Align text as you type

1 Move the cursor to the point where you want to type.

2 Click on the appropriate icon in the Formatting toolbar.

3 Text will be aligned accordingly from this point forward.

Copy formatting from one object to another

Text

1 Highlight the text whose Formatting you want to copy.

2 Click on the formatting toolbar.

3 Click and drag over the text that you want to apply the formatting to.

4 Release the mouse.

Colour scheme

1 Switch to Slide Sorter View.

2 Click to select the slide whose colour scheme you want to copy.

3 Click on the Formatting toolbar.

4 Click on the slide that you want to apply the colour scheme to.

Editing

Find text within a presentation

In a large presentation, you can quickly lose a word, sentence or paragraph. The **Find** function will help you to locate it.

1 In the **Edit** menu, select **Find**.

2 Enter some/all of the text you are looking for.

3 Click **Find Next**.

4 Continue to click **Find Next** until you find the text you are looking for.

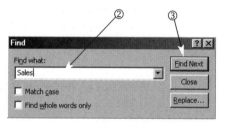

tip

You can search in part of a presentation only. Highlight the part of the presentation that you want to search in before following steps 1–4.

Replace words in a presentation

1 In the **Edit** menu, select **Replace**.

2 Type the text to be replaced into the **Find what** field.

3 Type the replacement text into the **Replace with** field.

4 Click **Replace All** to replace all instances of the text.

   OR

   Click on **Find Next** to locate the first instance of the text to be replaced. Click **Replace**.

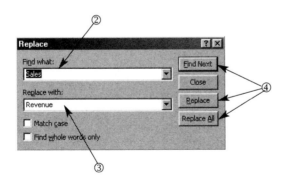

Undo an action

1 Click  to undo the most recent action you have performed.

2 Keep clicking to undo each preceding action one at a time.

3 Click the downward-pointing arrow to the right of to view a complete list of actions that you can undo.

Bullets and Numbering
Typing
AutoCorrect
Typing
Typing
Insert Text Box
Undo 1 Action

Restore an action you have undone

1 Click ↷.

2 Keep clicking ↷ to restore actions one at a time.

3 Click the downward-pointing arrow to the right of ↷ to view a complete list of actions that you can redo.

Proofing

Check spelling and style as you type

1 In the **Tools** menu, select **Options**.

2 Click on the **Spelling and Style** tab.

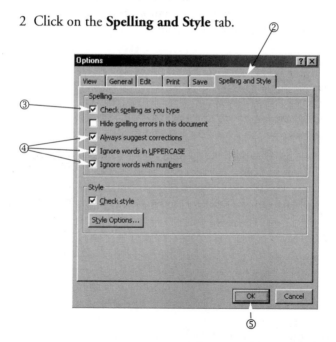

3 Place a tick in **Check spelling as you type**.

4 Select any other spelling or style options.

5 Click **OK**.

From now on, PowerPoint will automatically place a wavy red line under words that it does not recognize, and a wavy green line under common grammatical errors.

Correct spelling or style

1 Right-click on a wavy red or green line.

2 Select the appropriate correction.

   OR

Select **Ignore All** (to keep the word as it is spelled in the document).

   OR

Select **Add** (to add the word to the computer's dictionary).

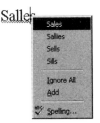

Correct spelling or style in a complete document

1 Click 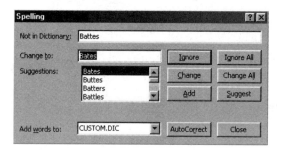.

   OR

   In the **Tools** menu, select **Spelling**.

2 Select an appropriate response to each error found.

3 Click **OK** when spelling check is complete.

Set spelling and style options

1 In the **Tools** menu, select **Options**.

2 Click on the **Spelling and Style** tab.

3 Select appropriate spelling and style options.

4 Click **OK**.

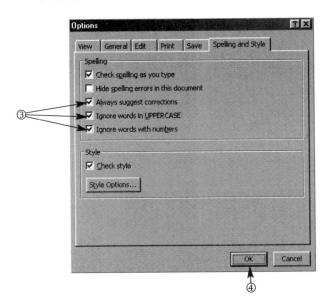

Rearranging Slides

Arrange slides in Slide Sorter View

1 Switch to Slide Sorter View.

Click and drag slide
to new positon

2 Click to select the slide that you want to move.

3 Hold down the mouse and drag the slide to the new location.

4 Release mouse.

tip

You can also rearrange slides in Outline View. See page 70 for more information.

Arrange slides in Outline View

1 Switch to Outline View.

2 In the View menu, point to **Toolbars** and select **Outlining**.

Click and drag this
icon to new positon

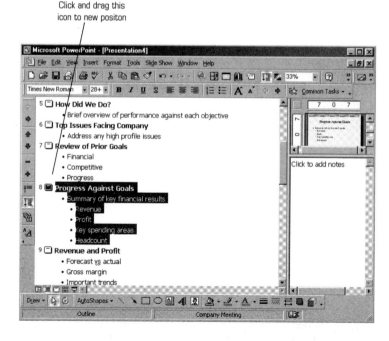

3 Click to select the slide number icon for the slide that you want to move.

4 Click where illustrated to move the slide up or down the slide order.

tip

You can also rearrange slides in Slide Sorter View. See page 68 for more information.

Slide Masters

PowerPoint includes features called Slide Masters, which enable you to control the formatting and positioning of titles and text in all slides within a presentation.

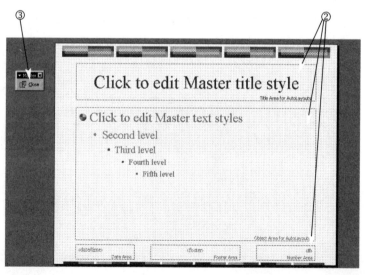

1 In the **View** menu, point to **Master** and select **Slide Master**.

2 Apply formatting and text changes that you want to appear in all slides in the presentation.

3 Click **Close** on the Master toolbar.

tip

You can insert a graphic image into the Slide Master, such as a company logo, so that it appears on every slide.

Title slide

Formatting that you apply to the Slide Master will affect all slides apart from the title slide. To make changes to the title slide:

1 In the **View** menu, point to **Master** and select **Title Master**.

2 Apply formatting and text changes that you want to appear in the title slide.

3 Click **Close** on the Master toolbar.

Notes Masters

The Notes Master enables you to create a consistent look and feel throughout all your accompanying notes pages.

1 In the **View** menu, point to **Master** and select **Notes Master**.

2 Edit and format your notes page as required.

3 Click **Close** on the Master toolbar.

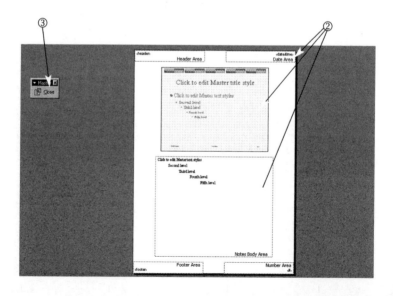

Handout Masters

1 In the **View** menu, point to **Toolbars** and select **Handout Master**.

2 Select the number of slides you want to appear on each page.

3 Make any other editing or formatting changes that you want to appear on all handouts.

4 Click **Close** on the Master toolbar.

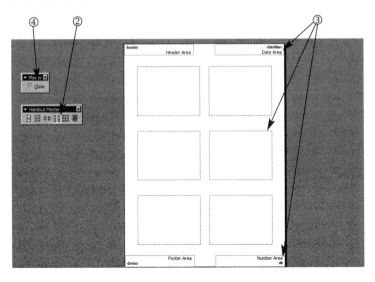

Insert slide numbering

You can display the slide number on every slide.

1 Click inside the text placeholder where you want the slide number to appear.

2 In the **Insert** menu, select **Slide Number**.

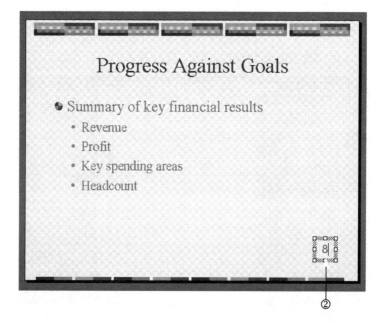

Change the slide start number

You may wish to begin your slides with a number other than 1.

1 In the **File** menu, select **Page Setup**.

2 Enter the slide start number where indicated.

3 Click **OK**.

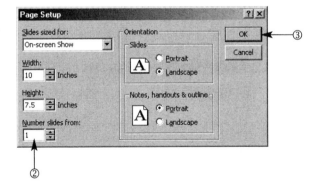

Insert date

You may wish to include the date on every slide.

1 Click inside the text placeholder where you want the date to appear.

2 In the **Insert** menu, select **Date and Time**.

3 Choose the date and time format.

4 Click **OK**.

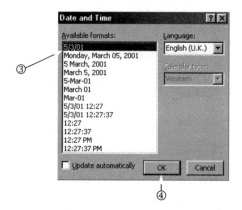

Add a header or footer

1 In the **View** menu, select **Header And Footer**.

2 Select either the **Slide** or **Notes and Handouts** tab.

3 Select appropriate header and footer options.

4 Click **Apply** to apply a header and footer to the current slide only.

   OR

   Click **Apply To All** to apply a header and footer to the whole presentation.

Colour

Select a colour scheme

1 In the **Format** menu, select **Slide Color Scheme**.

2 Click on the **Standard** tab.

3 Select the colour scheme you want.

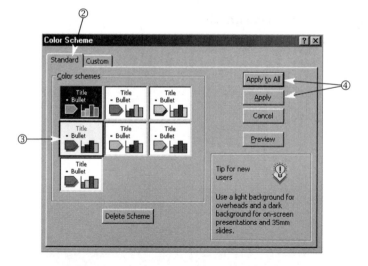

4 Click **Apply** to apply the colour scheme to the current slide

   OR

   Click **Apply To All** to apply the colour scheme to the whole
presentation.

Delete a colour scheme

1 In the **Format** menu, select **Slide Color Scheme**.

2 Click on the **Standard** tab.

3 Select the colour scheme that you want to delete.

4 Select **Delete Scheme**.

Apply the colour scheme of one slide to another

1 Make sure that you are in Slide Sorter View.

2 Click to select the slide with the colour scheme that you want to copy.

3 Click 🖌 on the Formatting toolbar.

4 Click to select the slide to which you want to apply the colour scheme.

tip

To apply the colour scheme to more than one slide, double-click on 🖌 before selecting the slides individually. Press **[Esc]** when you have finished to turn off the Format Painter.

Change slide background colour

1 In the **Format** menu, select **Background**.

2 Select a colour from the drop-down menu.

3 Click **Apply** to apply the background colour to the current slide only. Click **Apply to All** to apply the background colour to all slides.

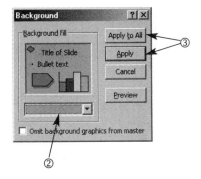

Choose a custom colour

1 In the **Format** menu, select **Slide Color Scheme**.

2 Click on the **Custom** tab.

3 Select the item whose colour you wish to change.

4 Click **Change Color**.

5 Click on the **Custom** tab.

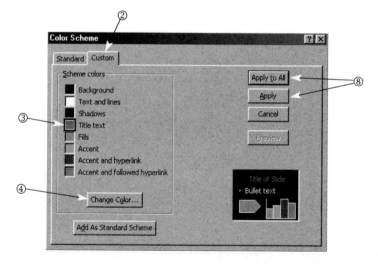

6 Click and drag on the palette to select the colour you want.

7 Click **OK**.

8 Click **Apply** to make the colour a part of the colour scheme for the current slide.

   OR

   Click **Apply to All** to make it part of the colour scheme for the whole presentation.

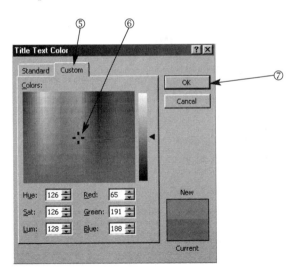

Save a colour scheme

If you want to save a custom colour scheme:

1 Choose a custom colour for each of the elements listed in the **Scheme Colors** list.

2 Click **Add as Standard Scheme**.

You will find your saved colour scheme featured next time you open the **Slide Color Scheme** menu.

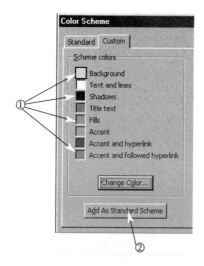

Change the colour of an object

1 Click to select the object.

2 Click on the drop-down menu next to the appropriate button on the drawing toolbar.

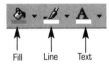

Fill   Line   Text

3 Click to select a colour from the colour scheme

   OR

   Click **More Fill Colors** to select from a wider range or to create your own custom colour.

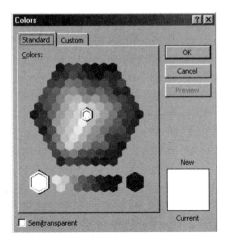

Change the colour of the slide background

1 Open the slide whose background colour you wish to change.

2 In the **Format** menu, select **Background**.

3 Click on the drop-down menu next to **Background fill**.

4 Select a suitable background colour.

5 Click **Apply** to apply the background colour to the current slide only.

   OR

   Click **Apply to All** to apply the background colour to the whole presentation.

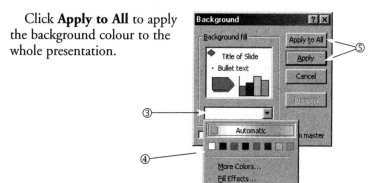

View a presentation in black and white

1 Click on the Standard toolbar.

2 Click again to revert to colour.

Print a presentation in black and white

1 In the **File** menu, select **Print**.

2 Choose **Greyscale** or **Pure black and white** where indicated.

3 Make any other print selections.

4 Click **OK**.

Effects

Select a background fill effect

1 In the **Format** menu, select **Background**.

2 Select **Fill Effects** from the drop-down menu.

3 Click on one of the tabs to see the types of effect available.

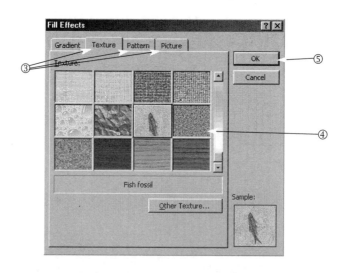

4 Click to select a fill effect.

5 Click **OK**.

6 Click **Apply** to apply the effect to the current slide.

   OR

   Click **Apply to All** to apply the effect to all slides in the presentation.

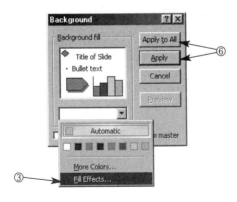

Apply a gradient fill effect

Slides can look very professional with a gradient colour effect.

1 In the **Format** menu, select **Background**.

2 Select **Fill Effects** from the drop-down menu.

3 Click on the **Gradient** tab.

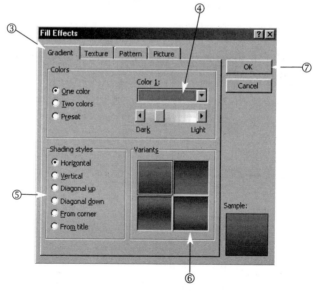

4 Select the colour(s) that you want to use.

5 Select a shading style.

6 Select the variant.

7 Click **OK**.

You can also apply fill effects to individual objects within a slide.

1 Click to select the object.

2 Select **Fill Effects** from the **Fill Color** drop-down menu on the **Drawing** toolbar.

3 Choose an appropriate fill effect.

4 Click **OK**.

Templates

Create a template

If you find that you often create similar looking presentations, you may want to create a template that you can use each time. You can create a template containing all the formatting, pictures and textual features that you want to appear in all the presentations that you create.

1 Open a new template.

2 Create all the heading styles, headers and footers that you want to appear.

3 Insert a logo or other graphic if you want.

4 Select an appropriate slide colour scheme.

5 In the **File** menu, select **Save As**.

6 Enter a suitable name for your template.

7 Select **Design Template** from the **Save as type** drop-down menu.

8 Click **Save**.

The next time you open the New Presentation dialog box, your template will appear under the **General** tab.

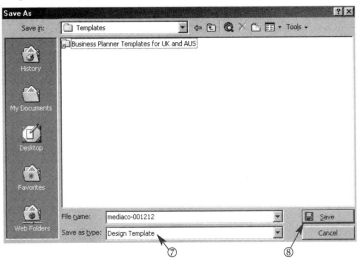

Edit/change an existing template

1 In the **File** menu, select **Open**.

2 Select **Design Templates** from the **Files of type** drop-down menu.

3 Navigate to the folder containing the template that you want to edit/change.

4 Click to select the template that you want to edit/change.

5 Click **Open**.

6 Make changes as required.

7 In the **File** menu, select **Save As**.

8 Select **Design Template** from the **Save as type** drop-down menu.

9 Click **Save**.

Apply a template to a presentation

1 Open the presentation that you want to apply the template to.

2 In the **Format** menu, select **Apply Design Template**.

3 Navigate to the folder containing the template that you want to apply.

4 Click **Apply**.

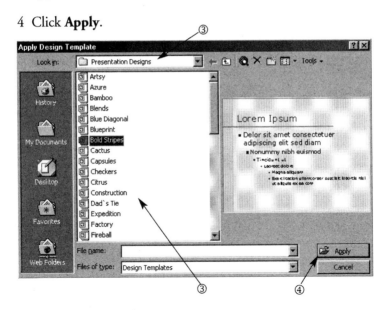

Add a template to the AutoContent Wizard

1 In the **File** menu, select **New**.

2 Click on the **General** tab.

3 Click to select the AutoContent Wizard and click **OK**.

4 Click **Next**.

5 Click to select the category in which you want your template to be displayed.

6 Click **Add**.

7 Navigate to the template that you want to add.

8 Click **OK**.

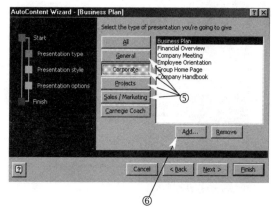

Apply the formatting from one presentation to another

Open the presentation that you want to apply the formatting to.

1 In the **Format** menu, select **Apply Design Template**.

2 Select **Presentations and Shows** from the **Files of type** drop-down menu.

3 Navigate to the presentation whose formatting you want to apply.

4 Click **Apply**.

Drawing

Display drawing toolbar

In the **View** menu, point to **Toolbars** and select **Drawing**.

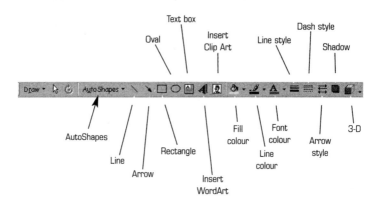

Text box

Oval

Insert
Clip Art

Line style

Dash style

Shadow

AutoShapes

Fill
colour

Font
colour

Arrow
style

3-D

Line

Arrow

Rectangle

Line
colour

Insert
WordArt

Nudge, snap, align or rotate drawing objects

1 Click to select the object.

2 Click on **Draw** on the Drawing toolbar.

3 Make appropriate selection from sub-menu.

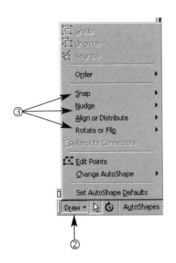

Draw/edit lines

1 Display the Drawing toolbar.

2 Click 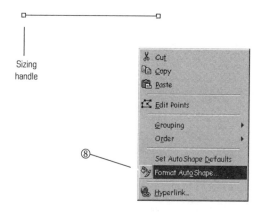 to select the line drawing tool.

3 Move the mouse pointer to where you want to draw a line.

4 Click and drag the mouse to draw the line.

5 Release the mouse.

6 Click on one of the sizing handles to resize the line.

7 Click and drag the line to move it.

8 Right-click on the line and select **Format AutoShape**.

9 Amend line weight and style, colour and size.

10 Click **OK**.

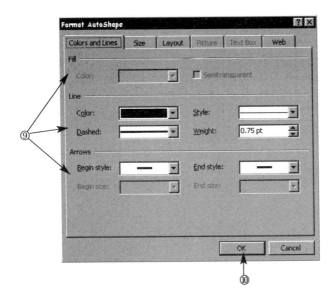

Draw/edit arrows

1 Display the Drawing toolbar.

2 Click ＼ to select it.

3 Move the mouse pointer to where you want to draw an arrow.

4 Click and drag the mouse to draw the arrow.

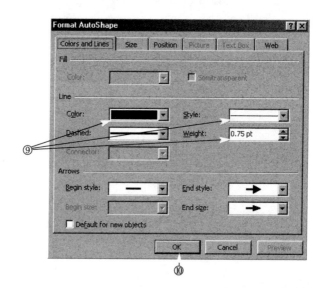

5 Release the mouse.

6 Click on one of the sizing handles to resize the arrow.

7 Click and drag the arrow to move it.

8 Right-click on the arrow and select **Format AutoShape**.

9 Amend arrow weight and style, colour and size.

10 Click **OK**.

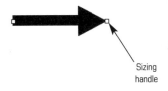

Sizing
handle

Draw simple ovals and rectangles

DRAWING

1 Display the Drawing toolbar.

2 Click on ☐ or ⬭.

3 Move the mouse pointer to where you want to draw your shape.

4 Click and drag the mouse to draw shape.

5 If you want to draw either a circle or a square, hold down **[Shift]** while clicking and dragging.

Draw AutoShapes

1 Display the Drawing toolbar.

2 Click **AutoShapes** to see the common shapes you can draw automatically.

3 Click on an **AutoShape** to select it.

4 Click and drag the mouse to create the shape in your document.

5 Release the mouse.

6 Click the shape to select it, and format it using tools on the Drawing toolbar.

tip

To keep the dimensions of the shape in proportion, hold down **[Shift]** while clicking and dragging the mouse.

Draw a freeform object

PowerPoint includes tools for drawing freeform objects and shapes.

1 Click on the **AutoShapes** button, point to **Lines** and select the freeform shape.

2 Click where you want to begin drawing your freeform shape.

3 Move the mouse to the next point in your shape, and click again.

4 Repeat until the shape is how you want it.

To stop drawing:

- Click near the original insertion point to complete the shape

   OR

- Double-click at the last point in the shape.

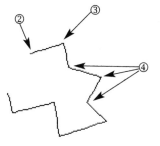

Draw a curve

1 Click on the **AutoShapes** button, point to **Lines** and select the curve.

2 Click where you want to begin drawing your curve.

3 Move the mouse to the point where the curve bends, and click again.

4 Create more bends using the same method.

To stop drawing:

- Click near the original insertion point to complete the bend

    OR

- Double-click at the last point in the bend.

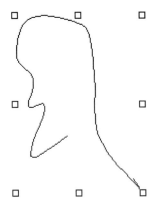

Resize an object you have drawn

DRAWING

1 Click to select the object.

2 Click and drag on one of the sizing handles.

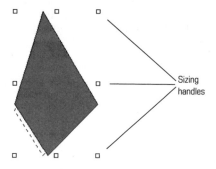

Sizing
handles

tip

To resize the object in proportion, click and drag on a corner
sizing handle.

Rotate an object you have drawn

1 Click to select the object.

2 Click 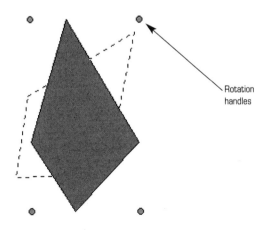 on the Drawing toolbar.

3 Click and drag on a rotation handle to rotate the object.

4 Click away from the object to stop the rotation.

DRAWING

Rotation
handles

Add a shadow to an object

DRAWING

1 Click to select the object.

2 Click 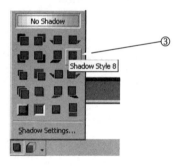 on the Drawing toolbar.

3 Click to select a shadow style.

Create a 3-D object

1 Click to select the object.

2 Click 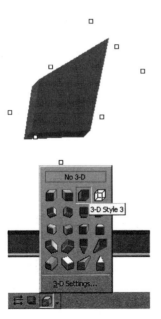 on the Drawing toolbar.

3 Click to select a 3-D style.

Group or ungroup objects

You may wish to group objects together, to make them easier to move or work with.

1 Hold down **[Shift]** whilst clicking individually on the objects that you want to group together.

2 Click on the **Draw** button, and select **Group**.

To ungroup a selection:

1 Click to select the grouped object.

2 Click on the **Draw** button and select **Ungroup**.

Multimedia

Find and insert a piece of Clip Art

1 Click in the slide where you want Clip Art to appear.

2 In the **Insert** menu, point to **Picture** and select **Clip Art**.

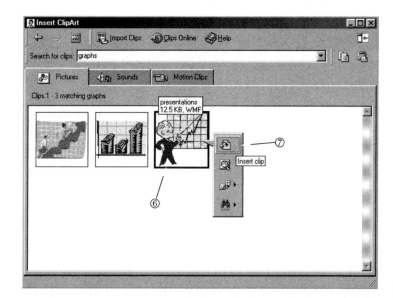

3 Click on the tab for the type of Clip Art that you are looking for (**Pictures**, **Sounds** or **Motion Clips**).

4 Type suitable keywords to locate the clip you are looking for.

5 Press **[Enter]**. A range of matching clips will be displayed.

6 Click to select a Clip Art image.

7 Click **Insert Clip** on the pop-up menu.

8 Click **Close**.

Insert a picture from a file

1 In the **Insert** menu, point to **Picture** and select **From File**.

2 Navigate to the drive and folder where the picture file is stored.

3 Click to select the picture file.

4 Click **Insert**.

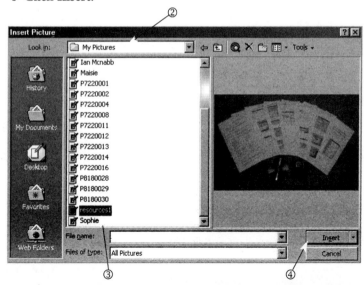

Insert a picture from a scanner or digital camera

PowerPoint is able to import pictures direct from certain scanners and digital cameras.

1 In the **Insert** menu, point to **Picture** and select **From Scanner or Camera**.

2 Select the appropriate device from the **Device** drop-down menu.

3 Select the resolution that you require.

4 Click **Insert**.

tip

If this feature does not work, you will need to import the photo or scanned picture onto your hard drive first, and then follow the instructions detailed in *Insert a picture from a file*.

Add a clip to the Clip Gallery

If you have an image that you plan to use regularly in your documents, it makes sense to add it to the Clip Gallery, so that it is always ready for use.

1 In the **Insert** menu, point to **Picture** and select **Clip Art**.

2 Click 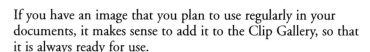.

3 Navigate to the drive and folder where the clip is stored.

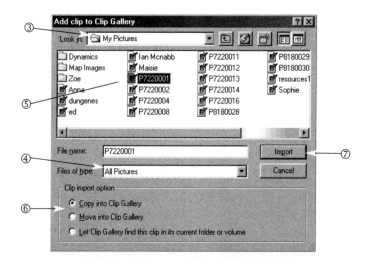

4 Make sure that you have selected the appropriate file type for the clip you are looking for.

5 Click to select the clip.

6 Select from the **Clip Import** options.

7 Click **Import**.

8 Select appropriate clip properties.

9 Click **OK**.

Insert a movie or sound clip

MULTIMEDIA

1 In the **Insert** menu, point to **Movies and Sounds**.

2 Select **Sound From Gallery**.

   OR

   Select **Movie From Gallery**.

3 Click to select the media clip that you want to insert.

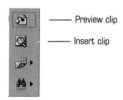

— Preview clip

— Insert clip

4 Select the **Insert Clip** button.

5 Click **Close**.

6 Select **Yes** or **No** to play the clip in the slide show.

Play a sound clip or movie

1 In Normal or Slide View, double-click the sound clip or movie icon.

2 In Slide Show View, click on the sound clip or movie icon once if it does not play automatically.

Sound clip or
movie icon

Edit a movie or sound clip

1 Right-click on the sound clip or movie icon.

2 Select **Edit Sound Object**.

   OR

   Select **Edit Movie Object**.

3 Make appropriate changes.

4 Click **OK**.

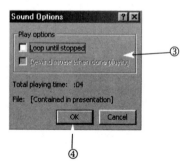

Record a sound

1 Open the slide where you want your sound clip to be heard.

2 In the **Insert** menu, point to **Movies and Sounds**, and select **Record Sound**.

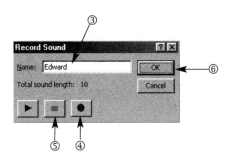

3 Give the recording a name.

4 Click **Record** button and make your recording.

5 Click **Stop** button when you have finished.

6 Click **OK**.

The 🔊 icon will appear on the slide. Double-click it to play the sound.

Pictures

Resize a picture/object

1 Click to select the object that you want to resize.

2 Click and drag on one of the sizing handles to increase or decrease the size of the object.

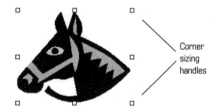

Corner
sizing
handles

tip

To keep the object's shape in proportion, click and drag a corner sizing handle.

Adjust the contrast of a picture/object

1 Click to select the object.

2 Click on one of the contrast buttons on the Picture toolbar.

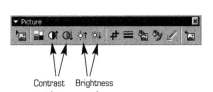

Contrast   Brightness
+/-   +/-

Adjust the brightness of a picture/object

1 Click to select the object.

2 Click on one of the brightness buttons on the Picture toolbar.

Make other changes to a picture/object

 PICTURES

1 Click to select the picture/object.

2 Click the appropriate icon on the Picture toolbar.

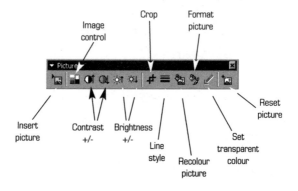

Image control

Crop

Format picture

Reset picture

Insert picture

Contrast +/-

Brightness +/-

Line style

Recolour picture

Set transparent colour

Give a picture/object a transparent background

1 Click to select the object.

2 Click ✎ on the Picture toolbar.

3 Move the mouse pointer over the object until it changes shape.

4 Click to select a colour that you want to set as transparent.

5 The chosen colour will now be transparent.

6 Click outside the object when you are finished.

Crop a picture

1 Click to select the picture that you want to crop.

2 Click on the Picture toolbar.

3 Click and drag the sizing handles until the area you want to crop is framed.

4 Click outside the image when you have finished.

OR

1 Right-click on the picture and select **Format Picture**.

2 Click on the **Picture** tab.

3 Enter appropriate values in each of the **Crop from** fields.

4 Click **OK**.

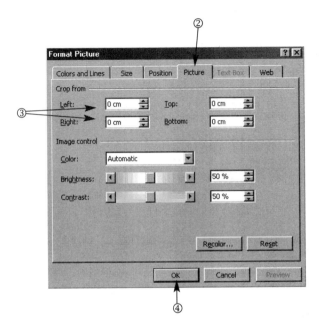

Tables

Insert a table into a slide

1 Open the slide in which you want to insert a table.

2 Click 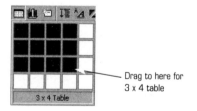 on the main toolbar.

3 Drag across to select the number of rows and columns you require.

Drag to here for 3 x 4 table

3 x 4 Table

4 Release the mouse.

5 Enter, edit and format text within the table.

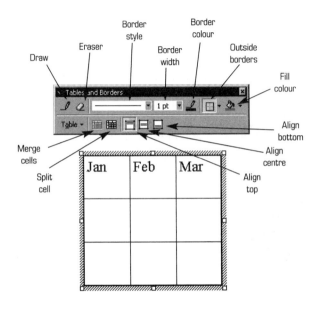

Insert/delete rows or columns

1 Click inside a cell next to where you want to add/delete a row or column.

2 Click **Table** on the **Tables and Borders** menu, and select an appropriate option from the drop-down menu.

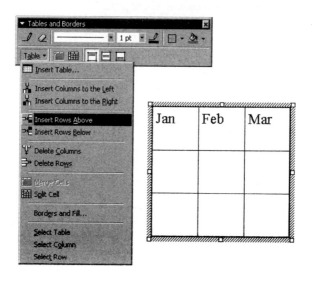

Make other changes to tables

1 Click to select table/cell/row/column.

2 Select the appropriate icon on toolbar.

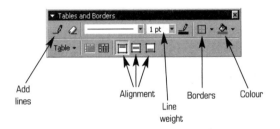

Add
lines

Alignment

Line
weight

Borders

Colour

tip

To adjust row/column width or height, click and drag on any table boundary until you achieve the result you want.

Object Linking and Embedding

Insert a file into a slide

1 In the **Insert** menu, select **Object**.

2 Click to select **Create from file**.

3 Click **Browse** and navigate to the file that you want to insert.

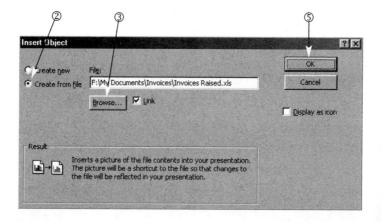

4 If you want to link the object, place a tick in the **Link** box. If you want to embed the object, un-tick the **Link** box.

5 Click **OK**.

Embedding a file

Inserts the contents of the file as an object into your presentation so that you can activate it using the application that created it.

Linking a file

Inserts a picture of the file contents into your presentation. The picture will be a shortcut to the file so that changes to the file will be reflected in your presentation.

Paste link an Excel worksheet

Paste linking is a very useful feature that enables you to place an object into a presentation, and keep that object synchronized with the original file from which it came. For example, you could insert an Excel worksheet containing sales figures, and the presentation would always remain synchronized with the original, ensuring that it is up to date.

1 Open the Excel worksheet.

2 Copy the item that you want to insert into your presentation.

3 Switch to the PowerPoint slide where you want the item to appear.

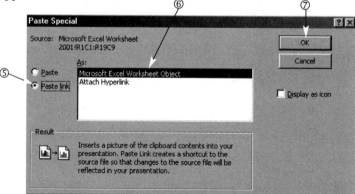

4 In the **Edit** menu, select **Paste Special**.

5 Select the **Paste link** option.

6 Select the appropriate object type from the list.

7 Click **OK**.

OBJECT LINKING AND EMBEDDING

Update links manually

1 Open the presentation with the linked object.

2 In the **Edit** menu, select **Links**.

3 Click to select the link that you want to update manually.

4 Click **Update Now.**

5 Click **Close**.

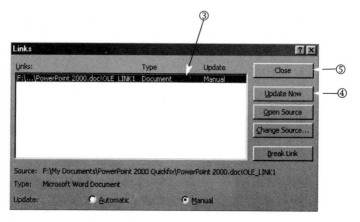

Break links

1 In the **Edit** menu, select **Links**.

2 Click to select the link that you want to break.

3 Click **Break Link**.

4 Click **Close**.

Insert a new Excel worksheet into a presentation

You can insert a new Excel worksheet, or any other Microsoft Office file, directly into PowerPoint.

1 In the **Insert** menu, select **Object**.

2 Select **Create New**.

3 Click to select **Microsoft Excel Worksheet**.

4 Click **OK**.

5 Edit and format the worksheet using the Excel tools displayed.

6 Click outside the worksheet to return to the PowerPoint slide.

EXCEL WORKSHEET

tip

You can insert a new Excel chart using the same method above.

WordArt

Insert WordArt

1 Click ![icon] on the Drawing toolbar.

2 Click to select a suitable WordArt style.

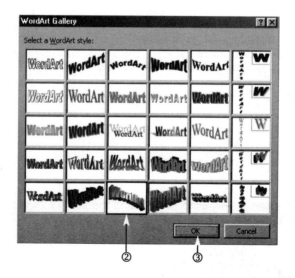

3 Click **OK**.

4 Enter your text in the space provided.

5 Apply any font formatting options that you want to use.

6 Click **OK**.

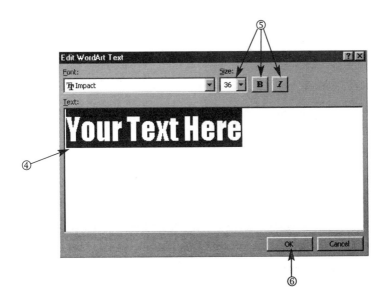

Edit WordArt

1 Click to select the WordArt text.

2 Click the **Edit Text** button on the WordArt toolbar.

3 Edit text as required.

4 Click **OK**.

Apply a new style to WordArt

1 Click to select the WordArt text.

2 Click on the WordArt toolbar.

3 Select a new WordArt style.

4 Click **OK**.

Change WordArt shape

1 Click to select the WordArt text.

2 Click 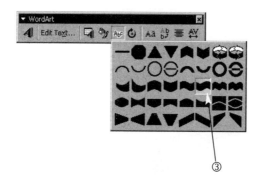 on the WordArt toolbar.

3 Click to select a new WordArt shape.

4 Click outside the shape to deselect it.

Rotate WordArt

1 Click to select the WordArt text.

2 Click ![rotate] on the WordArt toolbar.

3 Drag one of the rotate buttons until the WordArt appears how you want it.

4 Click ![rotate] again when you have finished.

5 Click outside the shape to deselect it.

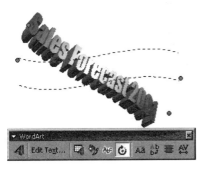

Give WordArt a different colour

1 Click to select the WordArt text.

2 Click 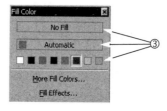 to select the **Fill Color** drop-down menu on the Drawing toolbar.

3 Select a new fill colour.

WORDART

Align WordArt text

1 Click to select the WordArt text.

2 Click ≣ on the WordArt toolbar.

3 Select an appropriate alignment.

4 Click outside the shape to deselect it.

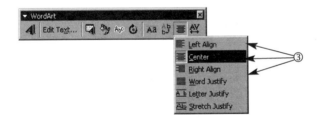

Make WordArt letters the same height

1 Click to select the WordArt text.

2 Click ![Aa] on the WordArt toolbar.

3 Click outside the shape to deselect it.

Change WordArt to vertical text

1 Click to select the WordArt text.

2 Click ![Ab] on the WordArt toolbar.

3 Click outside the shape to deselect it.

Change WordArt character spacing

1 Click to select the WordArt text.

2 Click ![AV] on the WordArt toolbar.

3 Select an appropriate character spacing.

4 Click outside the shape to deselect it.

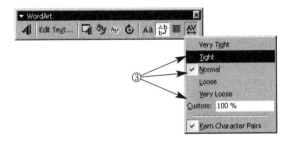

Charts

Insert a chart

PowerPoint comes with Microsoft Graph, which enables you to insert and edit charts directly in PowerPoint, without creating them first in another program such as Excel.

1 Open the slide where you want to insert the chart.

2 Click 📖 on the main toolbar.

3 Replace the sample data provided with the data that will be used to create the chart.

4 Close the datasheet to view the chart.

5 Click outside the chart area to return to the PowerPoint slide and menus.

Change the chart type

1 In the **Chart** menu, select **Chart Type**.

2 Select a suitable **Chart type**, and **Chart sub-type**.

3 Click **OK**.

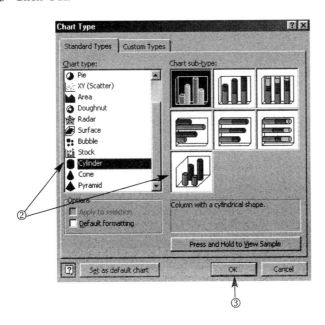

Format the chart

1 In the **Format** menu, select **Selected Data Series**.

2 Make formatting changes as required.

3 Click **OK**.

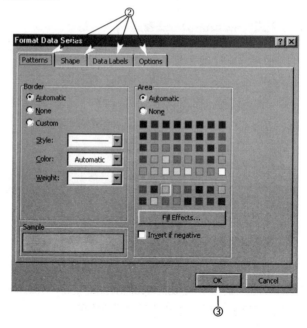

Import chart data

1 Open the chart in Microsoft Graph.

2 In the **View** menu, select **Datasheet**.

3 Click in the cell where you want the imported data to start.

4 In the **Edit** menu, select **Import File**.

5 Navigate to the folder where the file is located.

6 Double-click on the file.

7 Select the range of data that you want to import.

8 Click **OK**.

If you import data from certain applications, you may have to follow instructions from the Text Import Wizard.

Pulling a Presentation Together

Create a summary slide

1 Switch to Slide Sorter View.

2 Hold down **[Ctrl]**, then click to select the slides that you want to use for your summary slide.

Summary Slide

- Review of Key Objectives
  & Critical Success Factors
- Review of Prior Goals
- Progress Against Goals
- Revenue and Profit
- Key Spending Areas
- Goals for Next Period

3 Click on the Slide Sorter toolbar.

A new slide will be added, entitled Summary Slide, containing a bulleted list of the titles of the slides selected.

tip

Your summary slide can summarize all slides in the presentation. In the Edit menu, choose Select All before clicking on .

Insert a comment

1 Select the slide in which you wish to insert a comment.

2 In the **Insert** menu, select **Comment**.

3 Type your comment in the box provided.

4 Click outside the comment box when you have finished.

PowerPoint will automatically add your name to each comment that you insert.

Show or hide comments

1 In the **View** menu, point to **Toolbars** and select **Reviewing**.

2 Click on 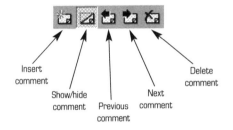 to show/hide comments.

Insert comment

Show/hide comment

Previous comment

Next comment

Delete comment

Delete a comment

1 Click on the comment box that you want to delete.

2 Click on on the Reviewing toolbar.

> **tip**
>
> To display the Reviewing toolbar: in the View menu, point to
> Toolbars and select Reviewing.

Format a comment

1 Click on the comment box that you want to format.

2 In the **Format** menu, select **Comment**.

3 Make appropriate formatting changes.

4 Click **OK**.

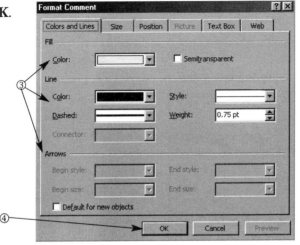

tip

To make formatting changes to the text inside the comment box, highlight the text and use the formatting toolbar.

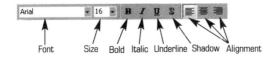

Embed TrueType fonts into a presentation

If you plan to show your presentation on another computer, you will want to be sure that the fonts that you use will be available.

1 In the **File** menu, select **Save As**.

2 Click on Tools ▾ in the Save As dialog box.

3 Select **Embed TrueType Font**s.

4 If you have not already done so, save your presentation in the usual way.

5 Click **Save**.

Replace fonts

1 In the **Format** menu, select **Replace Fonts**.

2 Select the font that you want to replace using the **Replace** drop-down menu.

3 Select the new font in the **With** drop-down menu.

4 Click **Replace**.

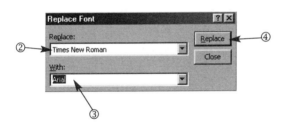

Change slide orientation

1 In the **File** menu, select **Page Setup**.

2 Select an appropriate orientation.

3 Click **OK**.

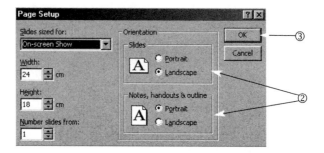

Include portrait and landscape slides in the same presentation

There is no easy way to include portrait and landscape slides in the same presentation.

1 Choose appropriate slide orientation for the majority of slides (e.g. Landscape).

2 Put the Portrait slides into a separate presentation.

3 Place hyperlinks into the main presentation, which link to the portrait slides.

tip

For more details about hyperlinks, see the section on *Web Presentations*.

Printing

Print a presentation

1 In the **File** menu, select **Print**.

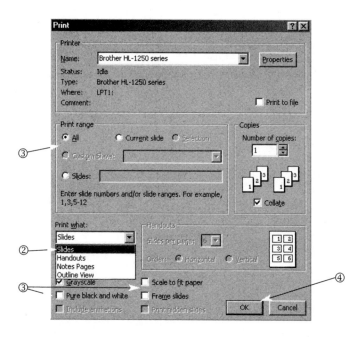

2 Choose what you want to print in the **Print what** drop-down menu.

3 Change any other print settings.

4 Click **OK**.

tip

You can print a complete presentation quickly and easily. Just click on 🖨 in the main toolbar.

Print a single slide

1 Click anywhere inside the slide that you want to print.

2 In the **File** menu, select **Print**.

3 Click on **Current Slide**.

4 Click **OK**.

OR

1 In the **File** menu, select **Print**.

2 Click on **Slides** and enter the number of the slide that you want to print.

3 Click **OK**.

Print a range of slides

1 In the **File** menu, select **Print**.

2 In the **Print range** dialog box, click on **Slides**.

3 Enter the slide range in the field provided.

4 Click **OK**.

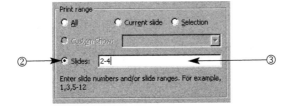

Print a custom show

1 In the **File** menu, select **Print**.

2 Select the **Custom Show** that you want to print from the drop-down menu.

3 Change any other print settings as required.

4 Click **OK**.

Select custom show from this drop-down menu

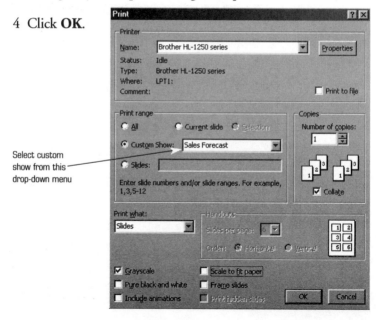

Print an outline

1 Switch to Outline View.

2 In the **File** menu, select **Print**.

3 Select **Outline View** from the **Print what** drop-down menu.

4 Click **OK**.

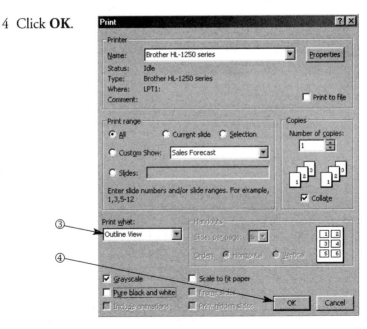

Handouts

Format handouts

1 In the **View** menu, point to **Master** and select **Handout Master**.

2 Click to select one of the handout options on the Handout Master toolbar.

Specify how many slides you
want to appear on the page

3 Add a header or footer if required.

4 Enter date and page numbering if required.

5 Click **Close** on the Master toolbar.

Add a header or footer to a handout

1 In the **View** menu, select **Header and Footer**.

2 Click on **Notes and Handouts** tab.

3 Enter header or footer text.

4 Click **Apply to All**.

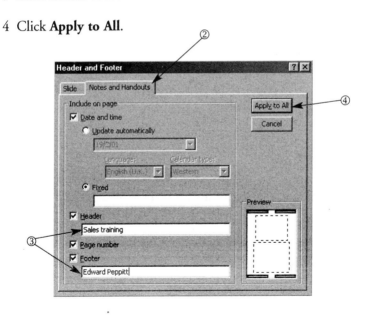

Print handouts

HANDOUTS

1 In the **File** menu, select **Print**.

2 Select **Handouts** in the **Print what** drop-down menu.

3 Select the number of slides that you want to appear on a page.

4 Select the handout order.

5 Click **OK**.

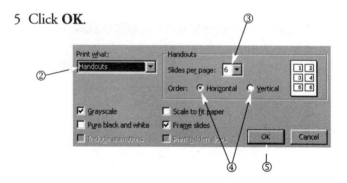

tip

To print each slide on a different page, select Slides in the 'Print what' drop-down menu.

Create handouts in Word 2000

1 In the **File** menu, point to **Send To** and select **Microsoft Word**.

2 Select the page layout option that you want.

3 Select **Paste link** if you want to link together the presentation and the Word document (to keep them synchronized).

4 Click **OK**.

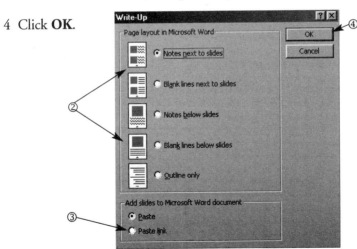

You can now edit, save or print the Word document in the usual way.

Speaker Notes

Prepare speaker notes

In Normal View

1 Open the slide.

2 Click inside the Notes pane towards the bottom of the screen.

3 Start typing speaker notes.

In Notes Page View

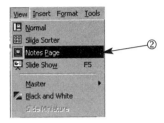

1 Open the slide.

2 In the **View** menu, select **Notes Page**.

3 Click on the text placeholder to activate it.

4 Start typing speaker notes.

tip

You can change the way that notes pages appear by
formatting the Notes Master. In the View menu, point to
Master and select Notes Master.

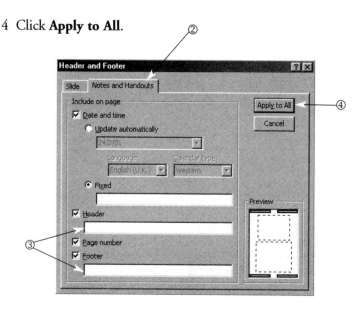

Add a header/footer to a notes page

1 In the **View** menu, select **Header and Footer**.

2 Click on the **Notes and Handouts** tab.

3 Add header/footer text.

4 Click **Apply to All**.

Restore placeholders to the Notes Master

You may wish to restore an item you have deleted to the Notes Master.

1 In the **View** menu, point to **Master** and select **Notes Master**.

2 In the **Format** menu, select **Notes Master Layout**.

3 Place a tick next to any elements that you would like to restore.

4 Click **OK**.

Change other elements of a notes page

1 In the **View** menu, select **Notes Page**.

2 Right-click inside the Notes pane.

3 Select the item that you want to format.

4 Make appropriate formatting changes.

5 Click **OK**.

Send notes to Microsoft Word

1 In the **File** menu, point to **Send To** and select **Microsoft Word**.

2 Make appropriate selection.

3 Click **OK**.

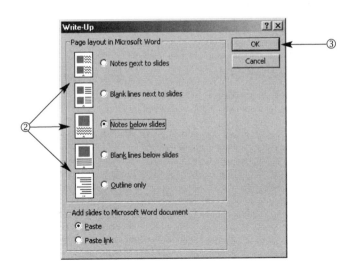

E-Mail

E-mail a slide

1 Display the slide that you want to e-mail.

2 Click 🖹 on the Standard toolbar.

3 Enter the e-mail address of the recipient.

4 Give the e-mail a subject.

5 Click **Send this Slide**.

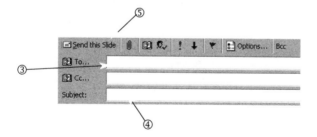

E-mail a presentation

1 In the **File** menu, point to **Send To** and select **Mail Recipient (as Attachment)**.

2 Enter the e-mail address of the recipient.

3 Give the e-mail a subject.

4 Type a message to accompany the presentation.

5 Click **Send**.

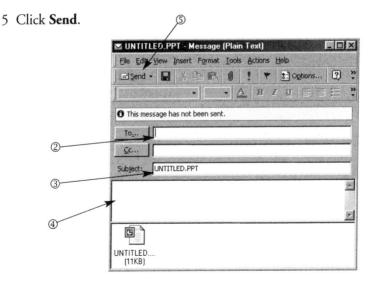

Web Presentations

Create a web presentation using a wizard

1 In the **File** menu, select **New**.

2 Click on the **General** tab.

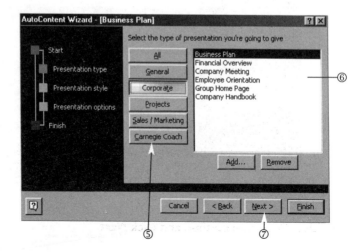

3 Double-click on **AutoContent Wizard**.

4 Click **Next**.

5 Click to select one of the presentation types.

6 Click to select an appropriate presentation.

7 Click **Next**.

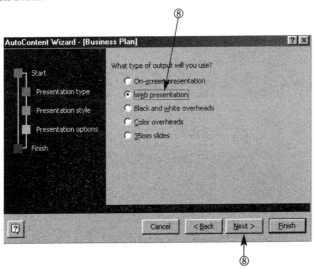

8 Select **Web Presentation**, and click **Next**.

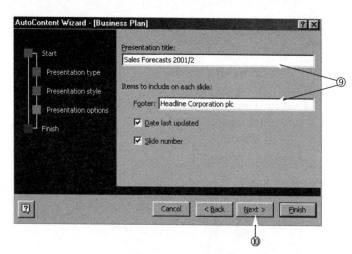

9 Give the presentation a title, and add any footer text as required.

10 Click **Next**.

11 Complete the remaining wizard fields.

12 Click **Finish**.

Create a home page in PowerPoint 2000

1 In the **File** menu, select **New**.

2 Click on the **Presentations** tab.

3 Click to select **Group Home Page**.

4 Click **OK**.

5 Edit the page as required.

6 In the **File** menu, select **Save As Web Page**.

7 Give the home page a file name and location.

8 Click **Save**.

Insert an action button

1 In the **Slide Show** menu, point to **Action Buttons** and select the action button that you want to use.

①

2 Move the mouse pointer to where you want to insert the action button.

3 Click and drag the mouse, releasing it when the action button is the right size.

4 Complete the appropriate action settings.

5 Click **OK**.

④ →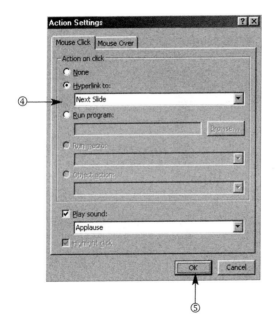

⑤

Turn an object into a hyperlink

1 Right-click on the object.

2 Select **Action Settings**.

3 Select either **Mouse Click** or **Mouse Over** tab.

4 Select **Hyperlink to** option.

5 Select a destination for the hyperlink from the drop-down menu.

6 Click **OK**.

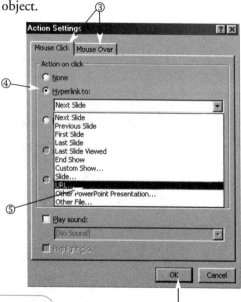

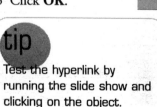

tip

Test the hyperlink by running the slide show and clicking on the object.

Create a hyperlink to another file

1 Right-click on the object in the slide.

2 Select **Action Settings**.

3 Select **Hyperlink to**.

4 Select **Other File** from the drop-down menu.

5 Navigate to the
file when prompted.

6 Click **OK**.

7 Click **OK**.

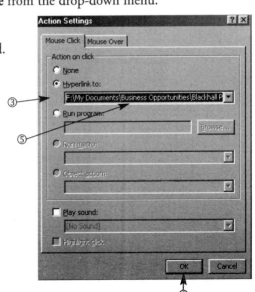

Create a hyperlink to a web page

1 Right-click on the object in the slide.

2 Select **Action Settings**.

3 Select **Hyperlink to**.

4 Select **URL**.

5 Enter the URL of the web page.

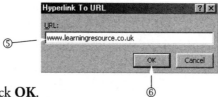

6 Click **OK**.

7 Click **OK**.

You can create hyperlinks to programs, presentations and
other files using the method described above, and selecting
the appropriate option in the drop-down menu.

Save a presentation as a web page

1 In the **File** menu, select **Save as Web Page**.

2 Navigate to the folder/directory where you want to save your web page.

3 Click **Change Title** if you want to change the title of your page.

4 Click **OK**.

5 Click **Save**.

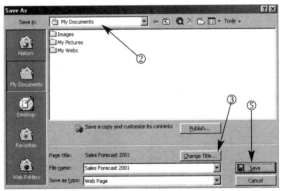

tip

When you save a presentation as a web page, the associated files are saved in a separate folder. If you move the web page, make sure you move this folder at the same time.

Save and publish a presentation as a web page

1 In the **File** menu, select **Save as Web Page**.

2 Navigate to the folder/directory where you want to save your web page.

3 Click **Change Title** if you want to change the title of your page.

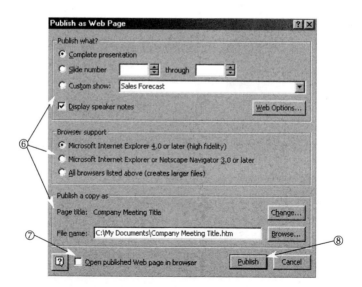

4 Click **OK**.

5 Click **Publish**.

6 Select from the options available in the Publish as Web Page dialog box.

7 Place a tick by **Open published Web page in browser**.

8 Click **Publish**.

Preview a web page

1 Open the presentation that you want to view.

2 In the **File** menu, select **Web Page Preview**.

3 Click **Close** to return to PowerPoint when you have finished previewing.

Slide Show

SLIDE SHOW

Set up a slide show

1 In the **Slide Show** menu, select **Set Up Show**.

2 Select the type of slide show that you want.

3 Select any other appropriate options as illustrated.

4 Click **OK**.

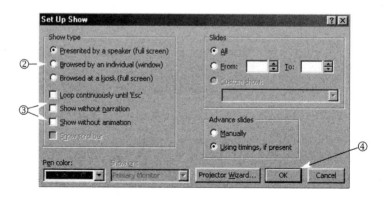

Show a range of slides

1 In the **Slide Show** menu, select **Set Up Show**.

2 Enter the first and last slide numbers in the range where indicated.

3 Click **OK**.

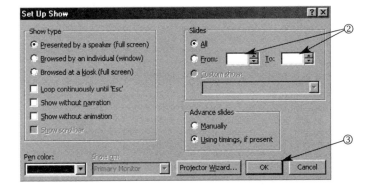

Hide slides

Make sure that you are in Slide Sorter View.

1 Click to select the slide that you want to hide.

2 Click 🔲 on the Slide Sorter toolbar.

Create a custom show

1 In the **Slide Show** menu, select **Custom Shows**.

2 Click **New**.

3 Give the custom show a name where indicated.

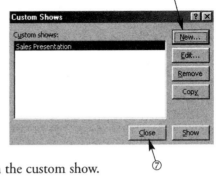

4 Double-click each slide that you want to appear in the custom show.

5 Select the order in which you want the slides to appear.

6 Click **OK**.

7 Click **Close**.

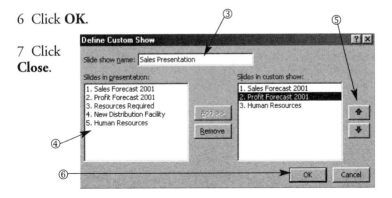

Show a custom show

1 In the **Slide Show** menu, select **Custom Shows**.

2 Click to select the custom show.

3 Click **Show**.

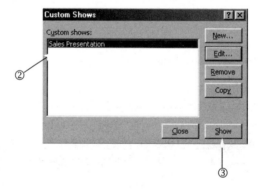

Edit a custom show

1 In the **Slide Show** menu, select **Custom Shows**.

2 Click to select the custom show that you want to edit.

3 Click **Edit**.

4 Add or remove slides, or change the slide order as required.

5 Click **OK**.

6 Click **Close**.

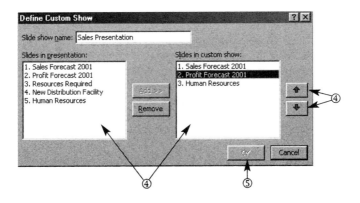

Create a slide transition

You can create a special effect when moving from one slide to the next.

Make sure you are in Slide Sorter View.

1 Click to select the slide to which you want to add a transition effect.

2 Select an effect from the **Slide Transition Effects** drop-down menu.

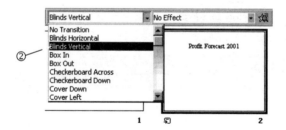

Apply transition effects to all slides

1 In the **Slide Show** menu, select **Slide Transition**.

2 Select an effect from the drop-down menu.

3 Click **Apply to All**.

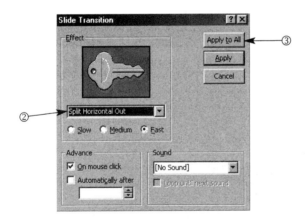

Set other transition effects

1 Display the slide that you want to add transition effects to.

2 In the **Slide Show** menu, select **Slide Transition**.

3 Make changes to the effect's speed, or add a sound to it as required.

4 Click **Apply** to apply the effect to the slide displayed only.

   OR

   Click **Apply to All** to apply the effect to all the slides in the presentation.

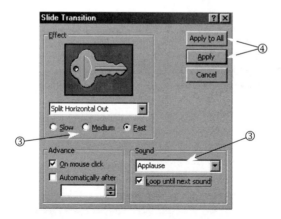

Preview transition effect

1 Display the slide whose transition effect you want to preview.

2 In the **Slide Show** menu, select **Animation Preview**.

Animations

Select a preset slide animation

PowerPoint comes preloaded with a number of automatic animation techniques, enabling you to add professional features to your presentation.

1 Select the slide that you want to animate.

2 In the **Slide Show** menu, point to **Preset Animation**.

3 Select the animation effect that you want to use.

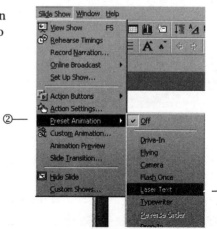

Create a customized animation

Make sure you are in Normal or Slide View.

1 Right-click an object in a slide and select **Custom Animation**.

2 Select the feature that you want in your custom animation.

3 Click **Preview** to see what your effect will look like.

4 Click **OK** when finished.

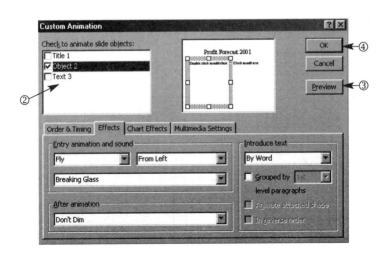

Use a text animation technique

Make sure you are in Normal or Slide View.

1 Select the text that you want to animate.

2 Right-click the highlighted text and select **Custom Animation**.

3 Click **Effects** tab.

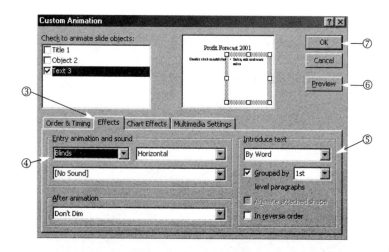

4 Select an animation effect from the drop-down menu where indicated.

5 Select an **Introduce Text** effect from the-drop down menu where indicated.

6 Click **Preview** to see what the effect will look like.

7 Click **OK**.

Animate bullets

Make sure you are in Normal or Slide View.

1 Highlight the bulleted list.

2 Right-click and select **Custom Animation**.

3 Click **Effects** tab if it is not already selected.

4 Select a suitable effect.

5 Click **Preview** to see what the effect will look like.

6 Click **OK**.

Dim text after animation

Make sure you are in Normal or Slide View.

1 Right-click text, and select **Custom Animation**.

2 Click **Effects** tab if it is not already selected.

3 Select a suitable dimming technique in the **After animation** drop-down menu.

4 Click **Preview** to see what the effect will look like.

5 Click **OK**.

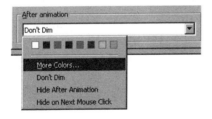

Change order and timing of animations

Make sure you are in Normal or Slide View.

1 In the **Slide Show** menu, select **Custom Animation**.

2 Click **Order and Timing** tab.

3 Edit order and timing of animations as required.

4 Click **OK**.

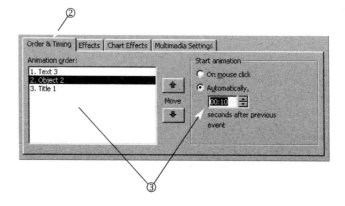

Remove animations

Make sure you are in Normal or Slide View.

1 In the **Slide Show** menu, select **Custom Animation**.

2 Clear the check box for any animation effect that you want to remove.

3 Click **OK**.

Final Preparations

Set time interval between slides

1 In the **Slide Show** menu, select **Slide Transition**.

2 Set a suitable slide interval where indicated.

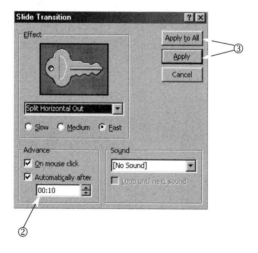

3 Click **Apply** to apply the time interval to the slide on display only.

   OR

   Click **Apply to All** to apply the time interval to all slides in the presentation.

Rehearse timings

1 In the **Slide Show** menu, select **Rehearse Timings**.

2 The slide show will begin. Rehearse the show, and press **[Enter]** each time you are ready to move on to the next slide.

3 At the end, click **Yes** to record the timings you rehearsed.

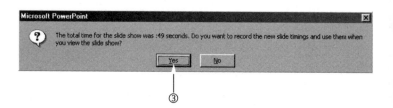

Test the timings you have rehearsed

1 In the **Slide Show** menu, select **View Show**.

2 Rehearse your presentation.

3 Check that the timings between slides are satisfactory.

Edit the timings you have rehearsed

1 Switch to Slide Sorter View.

2 Click to select a slide whose timing you want to edit.

3 In the **Slide Show** menu, select **Slide Transition**.

4 Change the setting in the **Advance** field.

5 Click **Apply**.

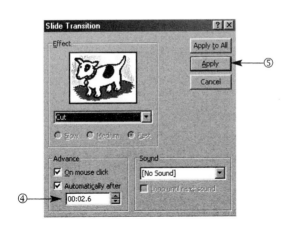

Record a narration

PowerPoint can record a narration to accompany your
presentation.

1 In the **Slide Show** menu, select **Record Narration**.

2 Set the microphone level as required.

3 Click **Change Quality** to select the sound quality you require
for your narration.

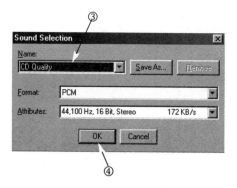

4 Click **OK**.

5 When the slide show begins, start your recording.

6 Continue your recording with each slide in turn.

7 At the end, click **Yes** to save your slide timings along with the narration you have recorded.

8 Run the slide show again to check the narration.

Presenting the Slide Show

Start a slide show

Click in the bottom left-hand corner of the screen.

OR

In the **Slide Show** menu, select **View Show**.

tip

You can call up the useful
slide show shortcut menu
by right-clicking anywhere in
the screen during a slide
show.

Go to a specific slide

When in Slide Show View:

1 Right-click anywhere on the screen.

2 Point to **Go**, then to **By Title**.

3 Click to select the slide that you want to go to.

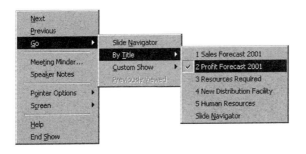

Go to a custom slide show

When in Slide Show View:

1 Right-click anywhere on the screen.

2 Point to **Go**, then to **Custom Show**.

3 Click to select the custom show that you want to go to.

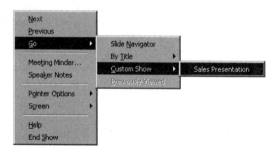

Turn mouse into a pen or pointer

When in Slide Show View:

1 Right-click anywhere on the screen.

2 Point to **Pointer Options**.

3 Click to select a pointer option.

tip

If you choose to turn your mouse into a pen, you can draw on your slides by clicking and dragging the pointer. You can also change the colour of the pen.

- Existing customers
- New customers
- New products

Create an action point

While you are presenting, PowerPoint allows you to record action points that arise.

1 Right-click whilst running the slide show and select **Meeting Minder**.

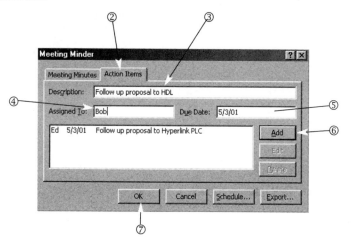

2 Click **Action Items** tab.

3 Complete the action description.

4 Assign the action to someone.

5 Enter a due date.

6 Click **Add**.

7 Click **OK**.

Create minutes

PowerPoint allows you to record minutes during the presentation.

1 Right-click whilst running the slide show and select **Meeting Minder**.

2 Click the **Meeting Minutes** tab.

3 Type minutes as they arise.

4 Click **OK**.

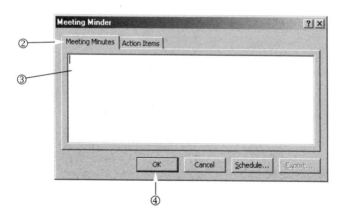

Export minutes to Microsoft Word

1 In the **Tools** menu, select **Meeting Minder**.

2 Click **Meeting Minutes** tab.

3 Click **Export**.

4 Select **Microsoft Word**.

5 Click **Export Now**.

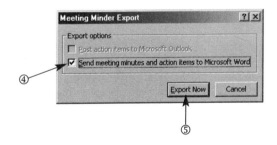

On the Road

Take a presentation on the road

PowerPoint allows you to pack up a presentation, including all formatting and fonts, and take it with you on a removable disk. You can then unpack it, and play it, on virtually any computer, whether PowerPoint is installed or not.

1 In the **File** menu, select **Pack and Go**.

2 Follow the Pack and Go Wizard instructions screen by screen.

3 At the last screen, click **Finish**.

4 Click **OK**.

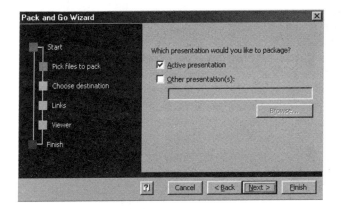

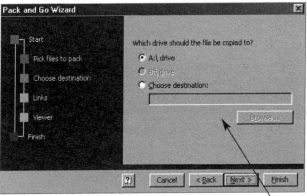

Copy file required to
pack presentation

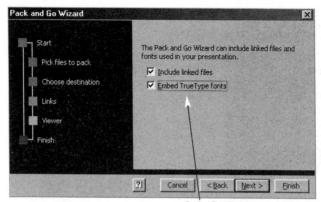

Embed TrueType fonts to be sure that your
presentation will look the same on any computer

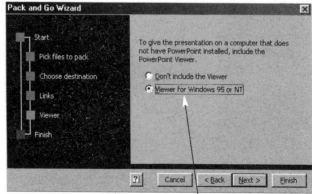

If you include the Viewer, you can run the presentation on any
computer, whether it has PowerPoint 2000 installed or not

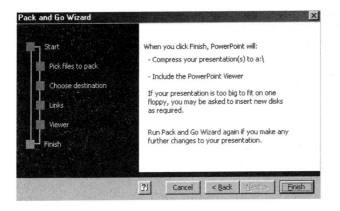

Unpack a presentation

1 Double-click on the file entitled **PNGSETUP**.

2 Choose a destination folder where the presentation will be unpacked.

3 Click **OK**.

4 Click **Yes** to view the slide show now.

Use the PowerPoint Viewer

The PowerPoint Viewer is a small program that allows you to view a PowerPoint presentation even if you do not have PowerPoint installed on your computer.

1 Navigate to the file entitled **PPVIEW32** and double-click it.

2 Locate the presentation in the **Look In** drop-down menu.

3 Click to select the presentation file name.

4 Click **Show**.

5 Click **Exit**.

Options

Change PowerPoint options

1 In the **Tools** menu, select **Options**.

2 Make appropriate changes.

3 Click **OK**.

VIEW
OPTIONS

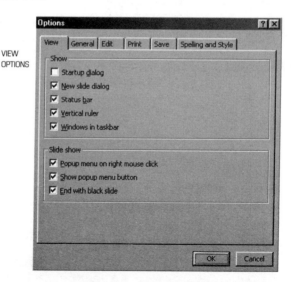

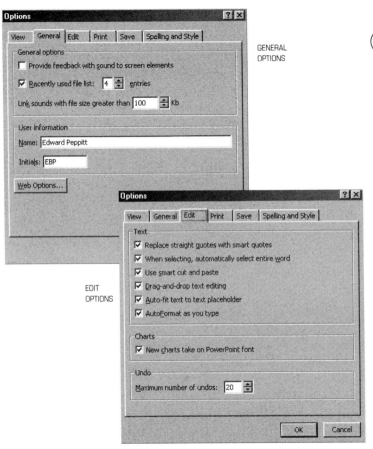

GENERAL
OPTIONS

EDIT
OPTIONS

Customize menu and toolbar options

1 In the **Tools** menu, select **Customize**.

2 Click the **Options** tab.

3 Change options as required.

4 Click **Close**.

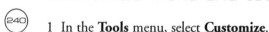

Customize

Toolbars | Commands | Options

Personalized Menus and Toolbars

☐ Standard and Formatting toolbars share one row
☐ Menus show recently used commands first
☑ Show full menus after a short delay

Reset my usage data

Other

☐ Large icons
☑ List font names in their font
☑ Show ScreenTips on toolbars
☐ Show shortcut keys in ScreenTips

Menu animations: (None)

Close

Create a toolbar

You can create a new toolbar, and add to it the buttons for the functions and features that you use most often.

1 In the **Tools** menu, select **Customize**.

2 Click the **Toolbars** tab.

3 Click **New**.

4 Give your new toolbar a name.

5 Click **OK**.

6 Click **Close**.

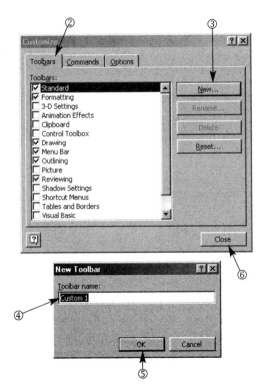

Add buttons to a toolbar

1 In the **Tools** menu, select **Customize**.

2 Click the **Toolbars** tab.

3 Double-click the toolbar that you want to add buttons to. The toolbar that you have selected will now be displayed.

4 Click the **Commands** tab.

5 Navigate through the **Categories** and **Commands** to find the button that you want to add to the toolbar.

6 Drag the button onto the toolbar.

7 Repeat steps 5 and 6 to add other buttons.

8 Click **Close** when finished.

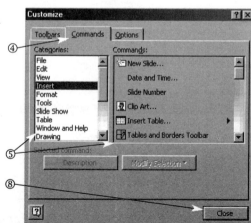